Stay-At-Home Mom's
Guide to Successful eBay®
Selling

Stay-At-Home Mom's Guide to Successful eBay® Selling

Suzanne Wells
Atlanta Golf Shop
atlantagolfshop@hotmail.com

iUniverse, Inc.
New York Lincoln Shanghai

Stay-At-Home Mom's Guide to Successful eBay® Selling

iUniverse books may be ordered through booksellers or by contacting:

iUniverse
2021 Pine Lake Road, Suite 100
Lincoln, NE 68512
www.iuniverse.com
1-800-Authors (1-800-288-4677)

ISBN: 978-0-595-43874-7 (pbk)

ISBN: 978-0-595-88197-0 (ebk)

Printed in the United States of America

Contents

1

What You'll Learn in This Book

Since I started my eBay business in 2003, I have sold thousands of items to thousands of buyers all over the world. During this evolving process, I have had numerous requests from friends, family, and other moms to share information about how to sell items and make money on eBay all from the comfort of home, and on your own flexible schedule. This guide will give you valuable information about the entire selling process. You'll learn:

- How to make thousands of dollars a month selling on eBay
- What to sell
- Where to find items to sell
- How to use eBay to its fullest potential
- How to take professional looking photos of your items
- Creative strategies for building your customer base
- Time-saving shortcuts
- How to fit eBay into your busy, stay at home mom schedule
- All about shipping
- Effective methods for growing your business
- How to get started TODAY, with no financial investment

This guide was written with stay at home moms in mind, but any motivated seller can benefit from the information.

As a stay at home mom, you have some flexibility to make an eBay business successful because you can arrange your own schedule. You can decide when you shop for, list, and ship your items. Most importantly, you can decide how much you want to work. An eBay business has unlimited potential as long as you are dedicated and persistent with growing your business. This truly is a business where the more you work, the more money you will make.

2

How my eBay Journey Began

My eBay journey began in 2003 after I went through a divorce. I was in the process of "cleaning out the junk," and was pondering a garage sale. The thought of having a garage sale made me feel tired! I have had garage sales before, and they are entirely too much work for the return. A few friends at work were hooked on eBay, so I thought I would give it a try. If they could do it, so could I.

First, I bought a few things on eBay to learn about the process. Everything went well and I enjoyed the experience. I borrowed a neighbor's digital camera and started creating my listings to sell my own items. At first, I sold quite a few items that were just lying around the house. Some examples include:

- A Dale Earnhardt car seat (sold for $71)
- An ugly bowl that I received as a wedding gift 15 years earlier (sold for $51)
- A used Kitchen Aid stand mixer (sold for $101)
- An old, gently used electric blanket (sold for $30)
- A collection of used high-end kitchen gadgets (sold for $42)
- A bottle (partially used) of expensive perfume (sold for $32)
- An old, broken, crystal clock (sold for $28)

The list goes on. Once I ran out of items from my own home, I realized that I had better find more things to sell. I was beginning to enjoy that extra income.

3

*What to Sell
and Where to Find It*

This section will cover some of the most frequently asked questions about what items to sell and where to find them.

How much money can I make?

I'll start by saying that eBay has not made me a millionaire (yet), but it has made me a thousandaire. The first month on eBay, my profit was $200. By the third month, my profit was $1,000. Before long, my profit reached $2,500 a month. Then $3,500 a month. Profits continue to grow. It will take time to grow your business, and you have to be willing to learn, experiment, and be patient. The potential is unlimited.

What do I sell?

The most popular question I hear is, "Where do I find things to sell?" First you'll need to decide WHAT to sell. Do you collect anything or are you an expert on a specific subject? Do you have any hobbies? Are your kids involved in a particular sport? Do you have access to a supply of something unique or in demand? Try to find a product that you enjoy working with, are interested in, and have access to. In order to be successful, you must have a passion for the items you sell. eBay is one way you can really love what you do, if you love what you sell.

You may not have to purchase anything to sell. eBay has a section on specialty services where sellers can offer graphic design, calligraphy, event planning, and artistic services. If you are a skilled artist and can draw or paint, you could have buyers email photos to you to work from. Do you sew, knit, crotchet, or embroider? You can make custom gifts for buyers. Just make up a few samples, take photos of them, and post them on eBay to see what happens. The possibilities are endless.

Where do I get it?

There are many sources for finding your products. The easiest are garage sales, flea markets, church rummage sales, and consignment sales. Check for garage and yard sales in the more affluent parts of town. You would be shocked at how many people are living beyond their means, in debt up to their eyeballs, and have a garage sale so they can pay their bills! These are great venues to find children's items, electronics, kitchen items, and vintage items.

Look at off-price Stores.

Try shopping at off-price stores such as Ross, TJ Maxx, Marshall's, and Steinmart. Many brand name and designer labels are available at these stores. Don't worry if the item is out of season. You can list it now or later during the appropriate season. For example, once I found a gorgeous Christmas sweater at an incredible price in July. I sold it the next week, in the middle of summer. Some eBay shoppers are savvy enough to look for deals all year. Keep in mind that if you are selling internationally, the seasons may be opposite from ours in the United States. If you are shipping globally, someone somewhere in the world is living in the right climate to wear it or use it right now. People may be shopping for vacation apparel and these items aren't available in the off-season. For example, cruises are popular year round. Have you ever tried to find a bathing suit or nice sundress in January? eBay is the answer.

If you want to stretch your dollar even further, and are fortunate enough to know a senior citizen who can go shopping with you, find out when stores have Senior Citizen discount days. You can save an additional 10-25% off your entire purchase on Senior Citizen days at some stores.

Go to end of season clearance sales at department stores.

Sometimes you can find designer items for 90% off the original price. Department stores WANT to get rid of this inventory. As long as you can sell the item for more than you paid for it, you are on the right track. You'll be building your customer base and your feedback score.

Big Lots is a virtual treasure trove. You can find DVDs, CDs, candles, clothing, kitchen gadgets, and household items. Sign up for their on-line ad to be emailed to you weekly.

Look at the mall.

Put your kids in the stroller and take a walk around the mall for fun. While you are there, walk through the stores and look for the final clearance sections. You can find incredible deals at The Gap, The Limited, Bath and Body Works, Yankee Candle, Aeropostale, Abercrombie, Banana Republic, and Gymboree. In my experience, "mall stuff" sells quite well.

You can also try outlet stores.

If you are lucky enough to live near an outlet, you can frequently check out the clearance racks for bargains. Get to know the store manager and staff, and they might tip you off when a big clearance event is coming. Don't forget to save your receipts and inquire about the return policy. If items that you have purchased from a retail store don't sell, you can return them for your money back or store credit.

Don't forget member's clubs.

Member's clubs like Sam's, BJ's, and Costco offer all kinds of items at rock-bottom prices. They offer quality, name brand goods for a lower price than retail. Your profit margin may not be as high, but you can still offer a quality item and build your customer base and feedback in the process. I once had a comment from an eBay member who said, "You can get these pants at Sam's for $16." My response to that comment was:

- Not everyone has a membership to Sam's
- Not everyone wants a membership to Sam's
- Not everyone has access to a Sam's
- Not everyone likes to shop
- Not everyone is physically able to shop
    - Moms who have small children
    - Senior citizens
    - Physically challenged people

- Families with no vehicle or only 1 vehicle
- International customers don't have access to Sam's

That eBay member definitely made me think. His statement could be true of any item sold on eBay. Sure, this item is available at Sam's, but have you ever been in a Sam's on a Saturday? It is mayhem, especially if you have to take the kids with you. Many shoppers would rather sit at home in their pajamas with a nice, hot cup of coffee and check out deals on eBay rather than drag their 3 uncooperative kids down to Sam's just to buy a pair of pants. (I am one of those people.)

Finally, I didn't know that the product I was selling was available at Sam's, so that was another source for my purchasing my inventory. eBay buyers are not only paying you for the item, they are also paying for your time and effort in finding the item and making it available to them.

Things you already have.

Don't forget about your kids' items that they have outgrown, or lost interest in. Has your child ever begged you to do a sport or activity and then after the first week, decided that it wasn't for him? SELL THOSE ITEMS. Case in point: My son begged me to let him play football. We bought the equipment (used of course), the shoes, the Under Armor, the pants. He decided he didn't like getting clobbered at practice 3 times a week. So, no more football. I sold his equipment and accessories on eBay as a set. I actually made money on that deal. Many parents don't want to invest in new items for sports as they have faced this situation before. You can sell apparel, equipment, and shoes from activities like baseball, soccer, dance, gymnastics, cheerleading, tennis, and ice-skating. Don't forget about musical instruments. Look for these types of items at garage sales.

Halloween costumes are good sellers. Your child wears it once, plays in it for a week, and then it goes on the closet floor. Gather up those costumes and put them up for sale on eBay. Electronics, CD ROM games, Playstation and Game-boy games, and learning products are good sellers. I sold our Hooked on Phonics set when my kids outgrew it, as well as a Leapfrog system. (Teachers, home schoolers, and day care centers often pick up used educational products on eBay.)

Look for name brand kitchen items. Calphalon, Circulon, Pampered Chef, Longaberger basket, and Kitchen Aid are good sellers. Yankee Candle, Bath and Body Works, and name brand (department store) perfumes sell well, even if used. Look for cosmetics like Clinique, Mary Kay, Lancome, etc. Those "free gift" items sell well.

Whenever one of my kids outgrows a size of clothing, I sell it as a "lot." You won't make a million dollars selling used clothing, but your items will find a new home and you will add another feedback point to your score. I often start these listings at a penny—it keeps the bidding interesting, and it is fun.

Once your friends and family find out that you are selling on eBay, they will come to you with items to sell. They see you as their ticket to fast cash. I have sold Peach Bowl tickets for my dad, china for my mom, clothing and collectibles for my friends. You can strike up whatever kind of deal you want and keep a percentage of the sale, and you can build your customer base and feedback score with no financial investment.

Sell items in a lot or batch. When my son finished his "Land Before Time" phase, I sold all 8 videos in a lot. Take care of an item's packaging and save the boxes. When your child has outgrown or lost interest in the item, you can sell it on eBay. Keep up with those DVD cases, CD cases, shoeboxes, or Playstation game boxes. An item sells much better if you can include the package or box it came in, even if it is used.

If you are a new stay-at-home mom, and have temporarily left your career to stay home to raise a family, consider selling some of your own items that you won't need. Business suits, career apparel, briefcases, purses, costume jewelry, shoes, and anything else that you haven't used in a while. Remember the rule, "if you haven't worn it in a year, you probably won't wear it again." Take a look in your own closet and see what you can part with. Maternity clothes are good sellers (if you are sure that you are finished with them). You will be amazed at how many things you won't miss once you start selling them on eBay.

You can shop on eBay for other products to sell.

I do not use this approach because I personally like to touch, feel, and examine the product before I purchase it. I also like the thrill of the hunt when shopping for unique items. It keeps this business fun! If you want to buy items on eBay, pay attention to the shipping cost. Don't get sucked into a sale without checking the shipping fee. Also, find out if the product has been exposed to smoke or pets.

You don't want to open your item and find it has a foul odor and you can't resell it.

Don't be afraid to experiment and try new products. I have sold everything including DVDs, shoes, china, and lingerie. Make a small investment, and give the item a try. It may lead you to a product line that you haven't even considered.

4

Time to Start Selling!

Now that you have some ideas about where to find your items, what do you need to get started? I highly recommend that you sell a few of your own things before purchasing items to sell. This is an easy way to decide if eBay is for you without a big financial investment. You will also become familiar with how eBay works. Consider selling your own items as your on the job training period. If you decide to continue selling on eBay, there are a few essentials you'll need to get started. You might already have them at home right now.

- First, you'll need a digital camera. You don't need anything extravagant, just a camera that takes good clear pictures. (A section on taking photos will be covered later.) You can even borrow one from a friend at first if you don't want to invest in one.

- Get a postage scale. Even if you are not processing your own shipments at home, you'll need to be able to weigh items to quote shipping charges. You can go to www.usps.com to calculate shipping fees. All you need to know is the weight of the item and destination (country or zip code).

- If you are selling clothing or other soft goods, be sure to have an iron, ironing board, starch, fabric freshener spray and dryer sheets. You may need to spruce up some items before listing them. (Don't let that word IRON disgust you, at least you'll get paid for doing it now!)

- Open a Paypal account. 80% of eBay users pay by Paypal. (More on this topic later.)

The most important step you can take in preparing yourself to be an eBay seller is to educate yourself. Explore the eBay site and read the help section. Ask other sellers questions. Spend the morning in a bookstore reading eBay books found in the entrepreneur section. (If you find one you like, go home and look for it used on eBay.) Check the library on books about eBay selling. Buy inexpensive items and pay attention to what other sellers do after the transaction. (Be careful and don't blatantly copy another seller's store, descriptions, or photo. This is a serious eBay violation and you can be suspended for text or image theft.)

5

Using eBay to its Fullest Potential

You are paying eBay to expose you to millions of potential buyers for your item. eBay is giving you access to millions of buyers worldwide that you could not otherwise reach. That exposure is worth paying for. (You'd never get 100 million people to show up at a garage sale.) There are ways to stretch your eBay dollar.

Open an eBay store.

You may find great items for sale, but they don't always sell the first time around on auction. When you open a store, you can put items in STORE INVENTORY on a 30-day listing for only cents a month. These items show up on searches, and shoppers will look at them. Always put your UNSOLD items into store inventory immediately. If buyers can't see what you have, they can't buy it! eBay Stores also provides you with sales and traffic reports as well as a wealth of other features.

Rely on the eBay help index for information.

Everything you need to know about technical questions, eBay policies, and eBay services is there. Scan through the help index from time to time and educate yourself on all of eBay's options and features. If you have to email eBay support with a question, don't be shy. Ask what you want to learn about. They might take a day or two to answer, but they are very helpful and will usually send a link to where you can find the information you requested.

Use your About Me page for important information.

Most people use their About Me page to tell their life story or show family photos. Others don't use it at all. Your About Me page is a great place to explain your policies, shipping procedures, selling philosophy, and more. It is the only place that eBay will allow a link to an outside website, in case you decide to sell products on your own website in the future.

Use your item title for relevant words only.

Have you ever seen titles with phrases like "must see" or "L@@K" or "WOW!!" included? eBay allows 55 characters for your title. The title and your photos are all the advertising you get. USE THIS SPACE WISELY. Try to use all of the characters by including as much information about the product as possible. For example, if you are selling a pair of Stride Rite shoes, your title should read something like, "NEW NIB Stride Rite sandals size 10 pink." Experienced eBayers know how to use the search feature and you want to use key words and acronyms that will help them find your auction. If they can't find it, they can't buy it.

Make sure your spelling is correct. A browsing shopper might find a name brand item with its title misspelled, but shoppers won't find you on a search if your spelling is wrong. One incorrectly spelled word can cost you a sale.

Make your item descriptions, well, descriptive.

Include measurements, color, size, and fabric content, manufacturer, washing instructions, weight, texture and anything else you can think of. Use lots sensory adjectives to describe the item. eBay shoppers can't touch, feel, or hold the item, so you have to help them envision how wonderful it is. Anticipate what shoppers will ask and include that information on the listing. You'll save time in the future because you won't have to go back and take the item out of storage, examine it for the requested information, and reply to their email. Look up that item on the Internet and see how retailers describe it. I am not advocating that you plagiarize material from the Internet, but you can definitely get ideas by researching how the big companies describe their items.

If the item has a flaw, be honest and mention it, and show a photo of it. THE KEY IS TO BE HONEST. You can't fool eBay shoppers, they are sharp and they carefully examine their purchases. Many times, a small flaw is not an issue, and as long as you mention it, some buyers just won't care. This could even work in your favor. Case in point: I bought a beautiful sweater at a garage sale to sell on eBay, but didn't realize it had a hole in it until I got home. The hole was beyond repair. I listed it anyway. I mentioned the flaw in my listing and a buyer contacted me to ask if I had more damaged sweaters to sell. As fate would have it, this buyer was searching for sweaters to use as the material for making small dog sweaters. From then on, I kept her and her business in mind when I was shopping and we have now a great business relationship. There really is a buyer for everything.

You'll have a better reputation when you mention the flaw up front. You will also avoid the hassle of the return-refund process, and you won't risk getting negative feedback.

Use an image hosting service.

You can find them at www.auctiva.com, and www.sellersourcebook.com among other sites on the Internet. An image hosting service is a website that houses your photos and provides templates for your listings. The fee is nominal. You will be able to customize your listings and give your items a very professional, clean, appealing look. Image hosting is easy to use, inexpensive, and it makes listing your items fun and interesting.

List items in two categories.

eBay allows you to list an item in two categories for maximum exposure to potential buyers. For example, once I found an interesting, unique tie with a shark theme. It wasn't a designer tie. It wasn't a $100 tie. It was just unique. I listed it under CLOTHING AND ACCESSORIES/MENS/TIES, and also under COLLECTIBLES/ANIMALS/SHARKS. The shopper who bought the tie worked at a nature conservatory and his hobby was collecting unique shark items. He wasn't even looking for a tie; he was shopping for "shark stuff." This has happened many times. You won't want to list every romper with a teddy bear appliqué in the TEDDY BEAR COLLECTIBLE category, but when you find unique items, list them in two categories. You might be surprised at who buys them and why.

Use eBay sales and traffic reports.

Study these reports. You can find out:

- Number of page views
- Number of unique visitors
- Referring domains
- Most popular pages
- Most popular listings
- Store search terms

- Percentage of return customers

- Number of items with Buy It Now purchases

- Path reports (previous and next page reports)

- Top key words that drive traffic to your store

Analyze which items have the most page views and the most unique (different) bidders. Focus on those items. See what days have the most page views. See how many unique visitors browse your store on specific days. Keep your own records so that you can track your profit (eBay doesn't know how much you paid for an item, so they can't give you profit reports). Trends will constantly change, but you can refer to your traffic reports to track what items appeal to buyers.

Use all automation that eBay offers.

I have my automation preferences set up to send an email when:

- A buyer wins an item

- We receive payment for an item

- We have shipped an item

- A buyer leaves feedback

The only emails I have to answer are specific questions on items, international shipping questions, or refund issues. You can revise your email templates whenever necessary.

Use eBay cross promotion services.

You can manually link items to a listing if they are similar in some way and you want to promote them along with the featured item. For example, if you have several Disney items, you can code your cross promotions to show Disney items at the bottom of the screen. A shopper may click on these cross-promoted items and ultimately buy them. Make it easy for your buyers to see what else you have for sale! Don't rely on them to drift into your store and look around. Tell them what you have and provide links in your listings.

*Tip: Put your best items up for sale on auction, and put other items in your store inventory. You will save you money on fees in the beginning, and you can get a feel for what sells. You are already paying for an eBay store subscription, so fill up your store.

Use BEST OFFER.

When you move items into your store inventory, you have the option to ACCEPT OFFERS FROM BUYERS. This is a terrific feature. BEST OFFER gives shoppers the power to bargain with you, and it gives you the opportunity to sell more items. Let's say that you have a child's coat in store inventory at a fixed price of $10. It has been sitting there for a while. A shopper comes along and offers $8 for it. Certainly, you would accept their offer and take the $8. You have made another sale, will receive another positive feedback, and have created a relationship with another customer. The customer is happy because you accepted her offer. You have empowered that customer and made a sale at the same time. Everyone is happy.

Use WANT IT NOW.

Want It Now gives buyers the chance to ask for items they want or can't find. Sellers can then respond to these requests with eBay listings. IMPORTANT: only respond to posts if the item you have is an exact match to the description in the post. You don't want to send a bunch of junk mail to people.

- It's fast—browse current posts to find buyers ready and waiting for you!

- It's easy—save your search and eBay will email you when buyers ask for what you want!

- It's profitable—Need a buyer for that one-of-a-kind item?

Make it a habit to check WANT IT NOW on a daily basis. The sooner you respond to a post, the more likely you are to get the sale. Use the search feature as well as the browse feature. Want it now posts often end up in the wrong category due to user error, so don't rely solely on browsing. If you are checking new posts every day, sort the posts by date and you'll only need to look at the most recent posts to find new listings.

Become a Trading Assistant.

A trading assistant is an experienced eBay seller who sells other's items for a fee. Once you are registered, your user id will be placed into the Trading Assistant

Directory so that eBay members needing assistance can contact you. Most trading assistants work on a per item basis. There is no obligation to accept an offer to sell someone's item. The decision is up to you, as is the decision of how much to charge for your selling service.

A word of caution about selling items for other people: It has been my experience that people will place a sentimental value on items they want or need to sell. Clarify up front the minimum amount they will take for the sale price. Example: A friend wanted me to sell a vintage formal dress that she had worn in a wedding 30 years ago. It was hand crocheted, made with incredible detail, and she originally paid over $600 for it in the 1970's. The dress was very special to her, and she found it beautiful, unique, and part of a cherished memory of the wedding of a dear friend. She would not let it go for less than the $600 she paid for it. She assumed that since the item was vintage, and very special to her, that it would be just as valuable to a buyer. The dress did not sell. Lesson learned: an item is only worth what someone is willing to pay for it, regardless of how special it is to the owner.

What about Buy It Now?

eBay sellers have mixed opinions on Buy It Now. Some never use it because they like the exposure to potential buyers for the full length of the listing. I have a different approach, but you have to do your homework to get the most out of a Buy It Now listing.

Once you have been selling similar products over a period of time, you'll get a feel for how much they will sell for. If you don't know how much an item will sell for, do a search for the item on eBay under COMPLETED LISTINGS. This will give you any items matching your key words that have sold over the last 30 days. This is an excellent way to find starting price, buy it now price, number of bids, number of different bidders, and page views for the item. Remember, an item's value is determined by how much someone will pay for it, not how much you think it is worth. Searching COMPLETED LISTINGS is a valuable tool that will help you gain insight on how much an item may sell for.

I offer Buy It Now (BIN) on most of my items for several reasons. First, it is only 10 cents per listing to offer BIN. One item sold on BIN can pay for all the BIN fees for the whole month. There are a variety of reasons a buyer may use Buy It Now.

The buyer may need the item to give as a gift and time is running short. They need it now, so they want to buy it now. People may be buying items for trips, vacations, weddings, parties, or holidays and they simply do not want to wait for an auction to end. Finally, some people are impulsive buyers. They see it, they want it, and so I give them the chance to buy it immediately. I would rather see one of my auctions end early and get the sale, than to have the customer buy a similar item from another seller, just because he is impatient.

You can capitalize on procrastinators by offering BIN on your auction items. BIN is great to use around holiday time—Christmas, Mother's Day, Father's Day, and Valentine's Day. You can use it on 3 and 5-day listings as the holiday gets closer. Be sure to factor in shipping time so that your customer has time to receive the item before the holiday. Be careful not to short change yourself by putting the BIN price too low.

6

Building Your Feedback Score

You have probably learned that feedback is eBay's rating system that is an indicator of a member's reputation in the eBay forum. You'll want to build your feedback score since a high feedback score indicates experience, quality products, and good customer service.

Always use your store name when leaving feedback for others. For example, one of our automated feedback responses is, "Fast payment, easy transaction. Thanks from Atlanta Golf Shop." Why should you do this? It is another way to get your store name in front of a potential customer. Let's say a shopper is scanning through another member's feedback. She may see the store name on the feedback and think, "Wow that sounds interesting. I wonder what this place is." Out of curiosity she clicks over to your store, and maybe she buys something, or adds you to her FAVORITES and visits you later when she has more time. See how that works?

A word of caution on leaving feedback for others. **NEVER, NEVER, NEVER leave feedback for a buyer before he leaves feedback for you.** I do not consider a transaction complete until a buyer has the item in his hands and he is completely satisfied with his eBay experience. Some sellers leave positive feedback immediately after receiving payment. A buyer should be judged on more than if he pays promptly, like if he becomes difficult if the package is lost in the mail. I like to wait so that I have some recourse if the buyer leaves me negative feedback, or there is a problem once he receives the item. He may receive the item, make an unwarranted complaint, and threaten to leave negative feedback for me. At that point I can gently remind him to leave feedback to accurately reflect his experience with us, but that we can do the same for him. Usually, the buyer will think twice about the negative feedback threat, or just not leave feedback at all. You can circumvent negative feedback by leaving feedback only after your buyers have left it.

You will want to build up your feedback score to gain the trust of potential buyers. An easy way to do this is to buy items on eBay. You can buy inexpensive items that you'll actually use such as party gifts, children's clothes, kitchen gadgets, office supplies, and your shipping materials. I make it a habit to buy 2-3 items a month on eBay so that I can check on the competition. I can see how items are packaged, how quickly they are shipped, how professional the seller is, and I even get new ideas for my own store by being a customer in someone else's store.

*Money saving tip: Did you know you can buy grocery coupons and gift cards on eBay? Some sellers spend their time organizing and sorting the coupons so you can get coupons for the exact items you use every week. I bid on coupons for products that I can actually use and if I win these items, I make money on the deal because I can save a lot of money at the grocery store! This works in reverse, too. You could sell coupons that you don't use as a way to build your feedback score.

Oh, no! Negative feedback!

You have done everything right. You found a great item, taken a nice photo of it, written an accurate detailed description, sent professional emails to the buyer, and shipped the item promptly and securely. Then, you log on to check your eBay account, and BOOM! There it is. Someone has left you undeserved negative feedback. You are heartbroken. Now what?

First of all, this is not the end of the world. With negative feedback, it isn't a matter of if; it is a matter of when. It probably isn't your fault. The buyer may have had a bad day, lost his job, or had a fight with his wife. You have no idea what happened in his life that day. He impulsively takes it out on you because you are accessible and you can't fight back. He takes out his aggressions on the computer, and you are the recipient.

Don't rush right out and leave negative feedback for the buyer that says, "WHAT A JERK—AVOID THIS BUYER." This will only make you look bad. If you choose to leave negative feedback for him, keep it unemotional and professional. You can say, "Disappointed that this buyer didn't contact us first—we always refund!" Shoppers will look at your feedback and wonder what the negatives are all about. Make it clear that you are the bigger person and you will always handle problems professionally and be fair if given the opportunity. Don't be impulsive and slap a negative feedback on someone without thinking about how it will affect your reputation. Be careful what you say!

When you do get a negative feedback, be sure to leave a reply below it on your feedback profile giving your side of the story. For example, we usually say, "Customer did not contact us regarding problem. We always refund!" Shoppers will see that you were blindsided with this remark and that you are willing do whatever it takes to make the customer happy.

You must be proactive in taking steps to prevent negative feedback. Add a sentence to your listings, your About Me page, all email correspondence, and your packing slip stating, "If you are not satisfied with your purchase, please contact us prior to leaving feedback and we will issue a refund." You want to imply that if negative feedback is left without giving you the opportunity to correct the problem, that the buyer is not eligible for a refund. Furthermore, you want to satisfy your customer so that he is eager to leave positive feedback for you.

Maybe you did make a mistake. Maybe you sent the wrong size or missed a flaw on the item. In all fairness, a buyer should give you a chance to correct the issue before slamming you with negative feedback. We are all human, we all make mistakes. Unfortunately, a small percentage of eBay members are too quick to leave negative feedback at your expense. This is part of doing business. Be sure to block that member from bidding on any more of your items. You probably don't want to work with someone who isn't willing to let you correct a mistake.

7

Photographing Your Items

After you have learned how to use your digital camera, you will need to take photos for your listings. This isn't hard, but it does take some thought and planning

Have you ever surfed eBay and seen pictures of items taken on someone's kitchen floor, bed, or couch? My favorite was a wrinkled dress lying on someone's unmade, rumpled bed. All I could think of when I looked at that photo was, "I wonder what happened in that bed before this picture was made." Yuck. I quickly clicked away from that photo. I've seen photos of items where the seller's feet are in the picture. I remember a photo of a dress hanging from a tree in someone's backyard and it wasn't even on a pretty hanger. Their dog was in the background doing his business. It wasn't appealing.

You can make your photos look clean and professional by using a solid background. I use white or black foam core board. You can use poster board that costs 25 cents. Use whatever colors you like, but keep in mind that you want the item for sale to be the focal point of the photo. Crop your pictures so that nothing else is in the photo except the item and the solid background. Make sure your photo is clear and you have used good lighting. Sometimes, the photo won't turn out even after you have tried to edit it on your computer. Put the item aside, and retake the photo again. A good photo is a major factor in getting a sale.

You can also use your scanner to copy images to post on eBay. If you are selling CDs, DVDs, books, anything new in a package, or new in a box, try scanning it. You can show close-up detail of a fabrics or clothing. Experiment with this technique and find out what works for you.

If you want to get creative with your photos, look at how the big companies do it. Look through some of those catalogs you get in the mail for background ideas. If you are selling bath products, you could use a pretty fluffy stack of towels for a background. I've seen listings with scrap booking paper as the background. It is cheap, fun, and re-usable. Be creative, but keep your photos neat and free of clutter.

While you are at the mall walking around with your kids, pay attention to store displays. If you see something attractive that may work with the types of items you sell, think about how you can replicate the background at home. You can get lots of ideas by paying attention to what you see in a retail store. Use the big companies' ideas as a springboard for your own.

Pay close attention to the item in the photo. If you are finding items at a garage sale or flea market, they will be in less than stellar condition even if they are new with tags. Take time to iron or press items so they are not crumpled and wrinkled in the photo. Remove lint from soft goods. Put a coat of shoe polish on kids' shoes and boots. Clean hard goods with window cleaner or furniture polish, whatever applies. (But don't take the price sticker off; you want to say it is "new with tag" if possible.) Take a few minutes to make the item look as new as possible. You don't want your buyer to have to imagine what the item could like if it was cleaned up. The potential buyer can't touch, feel, or examine the product in person. You have to convince him that it is worth buying through your words and pictures. A picture is worth a thousand words, especially on eBay.

8

Listing Your Item

Many books on eBay selling tell you what days and times to post your listings. In my experience, anything can sell at any time. (As of this writing, I have sold 11,547 items.) Don't overlook holidays. Think about it—not everyone is with family and friends on holidays. Businesses are closed and there is nothing to do. Some people are at home alone, or at work with nothing to do, goofing around on the computer. They may surf over to eBay for a look. I sell just as much on Christmas, New Year's, and Thanksgiving as I do on any other day. Some people are just plain addicted to eBay and will compulsively shop every day if given the chance. Provide items for them to buy!

If you can post your listing at certain times, like when both kids are at preschool or during the baby's nap, use eBay's SCHEDULED LISTING feature. You can write up your listing, post your photos, and program your listing to start on any day at any time you want. eBay charges 10 cents per listing for this feature, but it can come in handy if you have to do all of your listing for the week on one day. Maybe you are having guests or leaving town on a trip and won't be available to post your listings. You can do it in advance. You can schedule your listings to start at different times throughout the week.

I find it beneficial to list new items every single day of the week. Some shoppers only come in to eBay on certain days—maybe their day off, or when their kids are at preschool. You want to expose yourself to new shoppers every day! Repeat customers will check on you frequently for new items. Make sure you have items available for sale.

9

Selling Internationally

Selling your items internationally is not as hard as you might think; it just takes some preparation. When you offer your products to worldwide customers, you expose yourself to millions more shoppers and buyers. Even if international customers don't win your item, their bids will help drive the price higher.

eBay and Paypal do all the translating and currency conversions for you. In the event that you are having trouble communicating with your customer, a great resource for working with international customers is www.freetranslation.com—an on-line instant translation service. Just type in what you want to say in English, and select the language that you would like your email translated into. Bear in mind that you will receive an exact translation that may not account for slang, dialect, or expressions. At least you'll be trying to communicate better with your customer and he will appreciate your efforts.

Include information about international shipping on your listing. Either state that you will quote a price on request, or list prices for particular countries. The more information you can provide up front, the more likely a customer is to bid on your item.

If you are confused about how to ship an item internationally, go to the post office and ask a clerk. He will show you the materials you need, how to fill out the forms, and explain the shipping options. Once you have shipped a few international packages, you'll be a pro. It's really easy. International shipping delivery time can take up to 30 days. Packages have to be processed through the destination country's Customs Service. If your buyer emails you after a week looking for his package, politely remind him that this process can take up to 30 days and to be patient. The package will usually surface.

Selling internationally can be a great geography lesson for older kids. When I am preparing my international packages, I ask my kids to find that country on the globe. It's fun when you've sold Uncle Bob's cowboy boots and then ship them to Australia. Who knew?

10

Collecting Payment

Paypal is definitely the preferred method for several reasons. First, buyers generally pay faster when using Paypal. If a buyer has to go purchase a money order, then mail it out; you won't receive payment for several days. Checks and money orders can be fraudulent, so I do not accept them. Paypal is an electronic system, there is a record of the transaction, and the funds are guaranteed. You also won't have to worry about having a business account at the bank to deposit checks and money orders into. The great thing about having a Paypal account is that you can transfer your funds to your bank account on-line, or just go to an ATM and withdraw cash. When you sell on eBay with Paypal, you can get paid every day!

If you have not received payment or communication from your buyer after 2 weeks from the sale date, go ahead and relist the item. Next, block the bidder from bidding on anything else from you. Don't be afraid to leave negative feedback for non-payers. Many sellers are afraid of retaliation if they leave negative feedback. Don't be. Let's look at the big picture.

You sold an item 14 days ago and your buyer hasn't paid and hasn't replied to your emails. You go to their feedback page, and see that they have a low feedback score but no negatives. You are afraid to be the first person to leave negative feedback. For all you know, this buyer has won 5 other items that he hasn't paid for, but no one has left negative feedback because they are afraid of retaliation. If they had left negative feedback, this member would have been suspended by now and you wouldn't be spending your time dealing with him. We have to work together as a team of sellers to keep the undesirables off of eBay. You certainly don't want go on a mission to leave negative feedback over every little issue, but don't be afraid to use it when appropriate, especially for non-payers. Odds are that this buyer has totally lost interest in eBay and he won't even see the negative feedback because he isn't coming back to eBay anyway.

11

1-Cent Listings—What's Up With That?

By now you have seen listings that start at 1 cent. You are wondering why someone would start an auction at a penny and how they could possibly profit from it. There are several situations where a 1-cent listing is warranted.

First, let's say you have had an item in your store inventory for several weeks or months. You thought it would be a good seller, or you wouldn't have bought it. Shoppers have asked questions about it, but no one has purchased it. You are a little disappointed but you are ready to get rid of it and move on. You put it up for auction starting at 1 cent. What is the worst that can happen? 1-cent listings drive buyers to your store, and then to other listings with higher starting prices. You get more traffic.

Second, 1-cent listings make the bidding fun and exciting. In some cases, the bidding can go higher than the price you had set on the item in your store inventory. Buyers get involved in the bidding, a bidding war ensues, ego kicks in overdrive, and by gosh, they simply will not be outbid! The price just keeps going up.

Third, let's say the item actually sells for 1 cent. In this situation, you have one happy customer. He has bought a terrific item for only a penny! He is happy with eBay in general, and this is good for all of us. He now gets to experience your outstanding customer service, your professional emails, and your fast shipping. You will get a positive feedback point. Maybe he will be back for more, and spend more money next time. Maybe he will tell his friends about the great item he got on eBay for only a penny. You probably won't lose money, but break even on your investment in this item, because you'll make a couple of dollars on the shipping.

Finally, let's say that you have found an item that you absolutely know will bring a high price. You have no doubt that this is a hot item. You can start the bidding at 1 cent. You will get lots of page views, and lots of shoppers looking at your store. You have just set up free advertising for yourself. Some of my hot items get 100-200 page views in 7 days. Some of these shoppers will go on to buy other items in your store. They may like your store and add you to their favorites and visit you again. 1-cent listings are a valuable, practically free marketing tool.

Some eBay members are constantly on the hunt for 1-cent listings. Even if the item doesn't sell, you'll get traffic to your store and get exposure to potential buyers.

12

To Refund or Not To Refund—That is the Question

I offer a 100% satisfaction, money back guarantee on everything I sell. I know, you are thinking, "How can I make any money if anyone can return anything at any time? Once I have a customer's money, I want to keep it!" Giving money back is a scary concept at first, because it sure feels good to make those sales. But, a money back guarantee is a way to increase sales.

First, shoppers are more likely to buy from you if you have a fair refund policy. They may never have to use it, but it gives them peace of mind that they can get their money back if they want to. You are giving your customers options and empowering them. Again, use the Internet. Look at how the big companies handle refunds and how their refund policies are worded.

Second, you can re-list the item again once it is returned. Just refund the customer's money, then go to eBay and look up the item in your archived listings. Click on RELIST, and you're done. Sometimes, the item sells for more the second time around! You can still get positive feedback from the first buyer, especially if you promptly process his refund and include a professional email thanking him for his business. They key is to make the customer happy and get positive feedback. Make them want to return to your store.

Third, customers may contact you about a refund but never follow through with sending the item back. You know how it is, you put the item in your car to return it to the store or take it to the post office, and six months later it is still there. I keep my refund policy simple. Refund for the purchase price only, no store credit. I feel that only offering store credit may make the customer feel trapped—that they do not have options if they can't find a suitable exchange.

The idea is to keep the customer happy. Less than 1% of sold items are actually returned to me each month. (I sell around 300 items a month, and only 2 or 3 ever come back.) Some customers who have made returns will come back for future sales because they know first-hand that you are an honest seller who stands by your policy.

13

All About Shipping

I ship my orders about 4 days a week. I try to ship an item no more than 48 hours after payment is received. I prepare all of my packages at home, and drop them off at the post office, or have my mail carrier pick them up. (You don't have to wait in line if you are dropping off items with postage affixed. Get some tubs from the post office. Place the tub with your packages in an empty window at the post office, and you're done.)

I strongly recommend that you prepare your packages at home through an on-line service such as www.usps.com, www.stamps.com, www.endicia.com, or even through eBay. You can prepare your packages at your leisure, on your schedule, even if the post office isn't open. You won't waste hours of your time each week waiting in line at the post office.

Any size package can be shipped Priority Mail, but the minimum fee is $4.05. Supplies for Priority Mail are free and can be picked up at the post office, or shipped directly to you, free of charge, through www.usps.com. I order them in batches of 100 so that I always have a supply on hand. If you are selling books, CDs, DVDs, or other media items, use media mail. Media mail is a special, lower rate shipping class used only for media products. You can charge your buyers less for shipping and increase your chances of getting the sale. (Media mail may take longer to reach the destination, so you may want to give your buyers a choice of shipping options on your listing.)

Here is my philosophy on shipping. If an item weighs 13 oz or less, it can be shipped First Class. I purchase my own shipping bags and use First Class for these lighter items. I can buy poly-mailing bags for a few cents each when ordered in quantity. I don't have to spend the minimum $4.05 shipping an 8 oz item just to get the free Priority Mail supplies. So, if you have charged the customer $4 shipping and it only actually costs $2 shipping, plus the 10-cent investment for the poly-mailing bag, you have still made a profit and you can keep your shipping fee reasonable. If you have an item over 14 oz and are shipping Priority Mail, use the Tyvek envelopes whenever possible because the boxes weigh more than the envelopes, and you will be paying more for the shipping if you use a box. I also like to keep my packages small enough to fit into a customer's mailbox. Boxes and packages can be stolen off porches and doorsteps. Sometimes, using a large box is unavoidable, just be sure to use insurance or delivery confirmation.

If you are shipping fragile or breakable items, you don't have to spend a lot of money on bubble wrap or packing peanuts. Use those plastic grocery bags that you have piled up in the laundry room. They are lightweight and good for wrapping and cushioning items. You can also use newspaper. If you feel like you have to use bubble wrap or packing peanuts, look for these items on eBay and buy them in bulk.

International packages must be handled through the post office. You'll need to complete a customs form (which takes about 2 minutes) to attach to the package. I ship international items by Air Mail Letter Post. It is just as efficient as and cheaper than Global Priority. You can find information on international shipping through www.usps.com and on eBay. International shipping isn't hard or complicated; it just involves a different procedure. You expose yourself to millions of more customers if you are willing to handle international shipping. International customers just love American products. Ironically, they also love products made in their home country, but it is cheaper for them to buy it on eBay and have it shipped to them, than to buy it in their own country!

*Tip: Avoid the post office on Mondays and Saturdays. Drop your packages in mailboxes or have your carrier pick them up on these days. USPS offers free pickup at your home. The post office is more crowded on Mondays, Saturdays, and the day after a postal holiday. Even if you are just dropping off, you can avoid traffic, parking, and crowds by staying away from the post office on these days.

How much should I charge for shipping?

Again, check what other eBay sellers are doing. Search for items similar to what you are selling and see what the average shipping fee is. Some eBay sellers can be obnoxious with their shipping fees, charging $8 for a CD, or $10 for a shirt. I recently encountered a seller on eBay who charged $29.50 for shipping on a pair of medical scrubs. I asked him if this was a typo and he replied, "No, you can get them for $35 either way." I felt like this was deceptive and he was counting on people bidding on the item without looking at the shipping charges. A rather deceptive way to do business. He had a lot of negatives on his feedback score and the major complaint was, "Charges way too much for shipping." Keep your shipping fees realistic and competitive.

Note: Charging unreasonable shipping and handling fees is a listing violation. Some members use this technique to avoid paying final value fees on their items, as final value fees are calculated based on the sale price, not on shipping fees. You can be reported and suspended for circumventing fees.

I set up my shipping fees according to the type of item and use flat fees instead of calculated shipping. This is easier and faster than having to weigh each individual item every time you are listing it. For example, if you are selling DVDs or CDs, put a flat rate of $3 (or whatever you decide) for shipping. It is less confusing for your customers and they don't have to take the extra step of clicking the CAL-CULATE SHIPPING button. Try to "spoon-feed" your buyers—make things as easy as possible for them and condense the number of steps they have to take to make a purchase. Some larger packages will require calculated shipping, but as a general rule, I don't use it.

It is fair for you to make some money on the shipping and handling fee. After all, you are spending your time packaging the item, using your gas to take it to the post office, and using your printer ink, labels, and packing materials. Keep your shipping fees competitive and offer a discount for additional items. A shipping discount will encourage shoppers to buy more items from you.

14

Customer Service

This is a short chapter. Our customer service policy is simple. Treat customers the way you would like to be treated as a customer. Just because you are a small seller on eBay, doesn't mean that your standards have to be any lower than a major retailer. Be honest about your products, be polite, communicate well, act professionally (even in uncomfortable situations), and treat your customers with respect. Happy, satisfied customers are the key to your success. Keep them happy, and they will keep coming back, and maybe tell their friends about you.

15

How to Fit eBay into Your Stay At Home Mom Schedule

The baby is crying, your 3-year old is drawing tattoos on his arms with magic markers, and your 5-year old is trying to see if Marine Corps GI Joe can really swim by flushing him down the toilet. The dryer is buzzing and the cable guy is at the front door. How can you possibly run a business with all of this going on around you?

Be organized and plan ahead. You're not going to be able to devote 12 hours a day to this business because you are a mom and there simply isn't time. You have too many other responsibilities. But, you can make time for eBay if you are organized.

Try to do your serious shopping without your kids, if possible. You will want to give shopping your full attention, as this is the time that you are selecting items to convert into cash.

For a more efficient workday, do similar tasks in batches. Do all your shipping at once. Set aside a time to prepare packages for shipment and prepare them in a batch. I prepare my packages first thing in the morning as soon as my kids have left for school, so that those orders go out in that day's mail.

I spend my day at home preparing items and taking photos, in between doing laundry, unloading the dishwasher, and running to the grocery store. I take the photos, edit them, and save them in batches. Examine your item and decide what you will say about your item as you are preparing and photographing it. Is it vintage? Is it new with tags? What is unique about it? What color is it? Brown, topaz, cinnamon, or milk chocolate?

At night, after the kids hit the bed, I hit the computer and post my listings. Again, I do this in batches. Set a goal for yourself—5 items a day, 10 items a day, 25 items a week—whatever works for you. Listing is the fastest part. It is quiet, I can concentrate, and I end the day on a positive note because I have just added new exciting items to my store.

16

Timesaving Shortcuts

You will need a space dedicated to your eBay business. You'll need to set up your computer, printer, scale, and a storage system for your products. I started off using plastic tubs. It wasn't elaborate but it kept the items secure and out of the way.

Don't reinvent the wheel every time you do something. You experience all kinds of situations with buyers when working on eBay. Keep a FORM LETTER file with responses to commonly asked questions, or for special situations. Every time you write something unique or original, save it for future use. If it was asked once, it will be asked again. For example, customers may ask you to email them when you get a specific item to sell in your store. You won't have time to do that. I use the following form letter in that situation:

> Dear Customer,
>
> Thank you for your inquiry regarding ITEM. Unfortunately, I do not have more of ITEM in stock at this time.
>
> Save time when returning to eBay for great deals by storing your favorite searches, sellers, and categories. My Favorite Searches lets you save up to 100 item searches for easy viewing. You can also let eBay automatically search for you and notify you by email when new matching items have been listed!
>
> **How to save a search**
>
> 1. To begin your search, click the **Search** button at the top of any eBay page.
>
> 2. Enter the keywords you want to search for in the box.

3. After you get the search results you want, click the **Add to My Favorite Searches** link, which appears at the top right and bottom left of the item list.

The search will now be stored in My Favorite Searches. Next time you want to run a Favorite Search, simply click on the link to see your search results.

Note: If you're running the same searches frequently, you can sort search results by "newly listed" so that you see **new search results** at the top of the page and save some time!

Once your searches are stored, click on **Edit Preferences** in My Favorite Searches to:

- Name your search
- Choose to be emailed new results from this search
- Choose how long (from 7 days to 12 months) to receive search update emails

Thank you again for your inquiry and we look forward to working with you.

All of this information was copied from eBay's help page. You may want to provide the link to where you found it. You have just given your customer some valuable information about using eBay, and you won't have to keep up with his wish list. He will appreciate that you took the time to educate him.

Along those same lines, keep copies of all of your photos. Organize your photos into folders for quick and easy access. If you do this business long enough, you will find the same items over and over again. (You'll be shopping and think, "I know I have sold this dress before.") When it is time to list that item, you will already have your own photo of it. You can also check your ARCHIVED LISTINGS and see if the item is still there. (eBay purges archived listings after a few months.) If it is in your ARCHIVED LISTINGS, you can just hit RELIST, make any minor changes regarding size or measurements, and you're done. You can also save listings of items to reuse in the future.

Keep a spreadsheet of your inventory. You'll know what you have, and most importantly, how much you spent. If someone asks you if you have a particular item, you can check your spreadsheet instead of having to sort through your stock to find it.

17

A Little About Marketing

eBay will do most of your marketing for you by exposing your items to millions of buyers. Have you ever tried to get 220 million people to come to your garage sale? You don't have to because they are just waiting on eBay for you. Be creative, have fun, and do other things on your own.

If you are good with Microsoft WORD or graphic design programs, you can print your own materials. I print my own return address labels and package labels. Make up flyers or advertisements to put in your orders. Pay attention to what is going on around you. If you get a sales flyer in the mail from Macys about a SUMMER CLEARANCE, create your own promotion along those lines for your store. Use words like CLEARANCE, SALE, INVENTORY REDUCTION, and SPECIAL OFFER.

Be prepared. Keep extra digital camera batteries on hand. The last thing you need is to find your camera batteries are dead at 10:00 at night and the kids are in bed. Great, you're stuck. You aren't exactly in the mood to run up to Wal-Mart to get batteries at this time of night so you can post your listings for the day. Have plenty of supplies like extra printer cartridges, labels, paper, and shipping supplies on hand. As a mom, you know it never fails that the kids get sick at the most inconvenient times. You have 20 packages to ship, and you have run out of Priority Mail supplies—your daughter wakes up the next day with a fever of 102. You can't leave to go out and get more supplies, and you sure can't take her with you. Realize that there are days you will be stuck at home with sick kids, so be prepared with plenty of supplies and inventory to list for sale so you can work while your child is resting.

Use eBay services to give your store a professional look. Did you know that you can buy services like logo creation and web page design on eBay? There are lots of creative people who offer these services at very reasonable prices. (Maybe you are one of them—you can sell your design services on eBay and you won't even have to buy any inventory!) Look for services sold on eBay and see what you can find!

Have business cards printed at www.vistaprint.com. You can get high quality glossy or matte business cards thru this website for a very reasonable price. Vistaprint offers a self-design process where you can create your own business cards to look any way you want. Vistaprint also offers other promotional items like magnets and flyers at very reasonable prices. Have cards printed and ask your friends and family to pass them out when appropriate. You can also include your business cards in your orders so that your customers can save them for future use, or give them to a friend.

18

The Bottom Line

eBay is not a get rich quick scheme. If it were, everyone would be doing it. Building an eBay business takes time, effort, organization, creativity, and diligence. Do your homework, and watch what other sellers are doing. Think, experiment, and keep your eyes open. eBay is your chance to express your creativity. Unlike any other job I have had, eBay gives you positive feedback every single day. How many of us have had jobs where the boss never has a word of praise for our efforts? On eBay, you will receive glowing comments and positive reinforcement that just makes you feel good. There is nothing more motivating than words of praise about your work.

eBay is the second most visited website on the Internet, has over 200 million members in over 150 countries around the world, and is easy to use. 80,000 new users register on eBay every day. You can reap the benefits if you are ambitious, patient, and willing to learn and experiment. Now go out there and get started!

*Disclaimer: We have prepared this report for informative purposes. This report in no way guarantees your success as an eBay seller. Suzanne Wells and Atlanta Golf Shop cannot be held liable for any loss or profit gained by reading this material.

Helpful Resources

www.bagmart.com for ordering plastic packaging of any kind

www.cartridgeworld.com for refilling and recycling printer cartridges

www.ehow.com how to do just about anything!

www.geeksquad.com help with your home computer

www.printpal.com for inexpensive printer cartridges

www.sellersourcebook.com for image hosting

www.usps.com for all of your shipping questions

978-0-595-43874-7
0-595-43874-1